THE SHAPE OF WATER

MUSIC FROM THE MOTION PICTURE SOUNDTRACK

ISBN 978-1-5400-2781-8

7777 W. BLUEMOUND RD. P.O. BOX 13819 MILWAUKEE, WI 53213

Visit Hal Leonard Online at
www.halleonard.com

THE SHAPE OF WATER

By ALEXANDRE DESPLAT

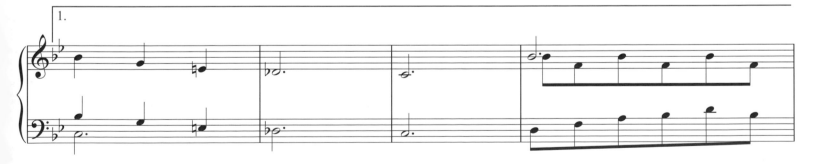

YOU'LL NEVER KNOW

Words by MACK GORDON
Music by HARRY WARREN

10

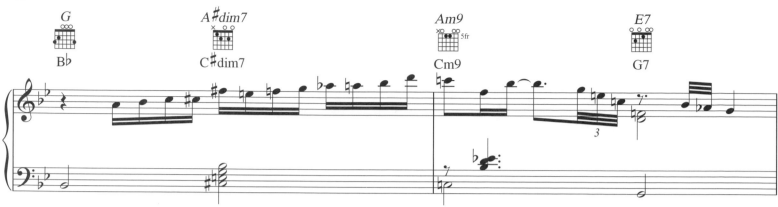

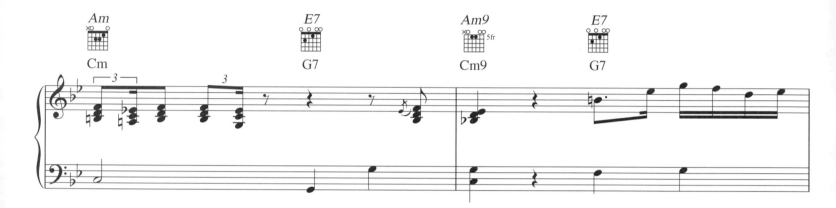

D.S. al Coda

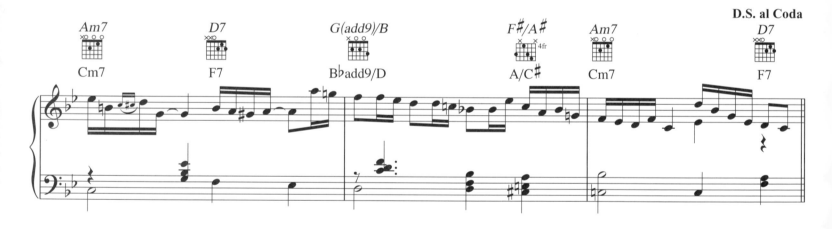

CODA

now.

rit.

ELISA'S THEME

By ALEXANDRE DESPLAT

ELISA AND ZELDA

By ALEXANDRE DESPLAT

Moderate Waltz

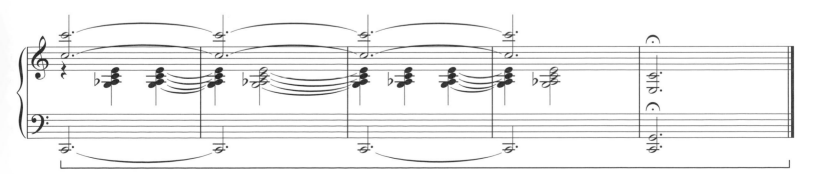

FIVE STARS GENERAL

By ALEXANDRE DESPLAT

Moderately

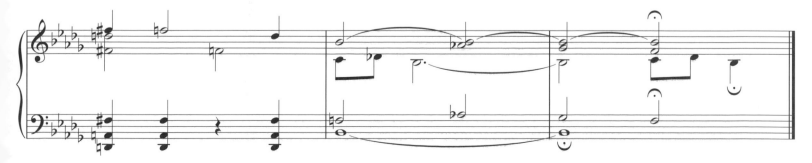

THAT ISN'T GOOD

By ALEXANDRE DESPLAT

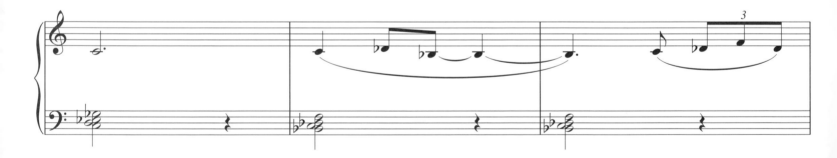

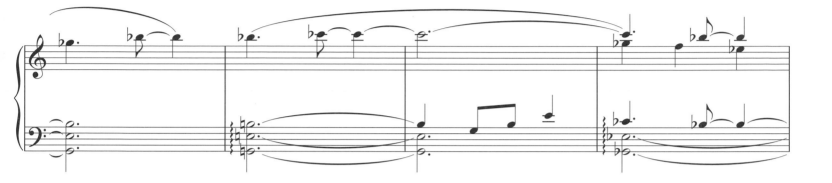

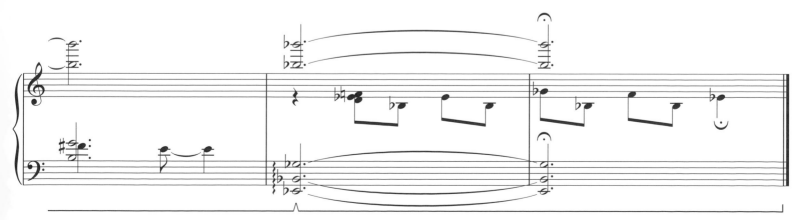

UNDERWATER KISS

By ALEXANDRE DESPLAT

Slowly, expressively

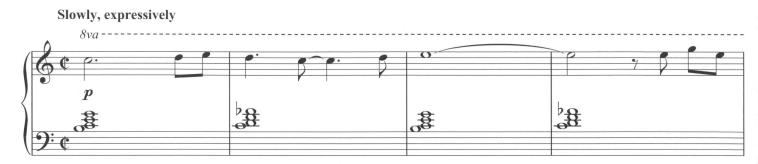

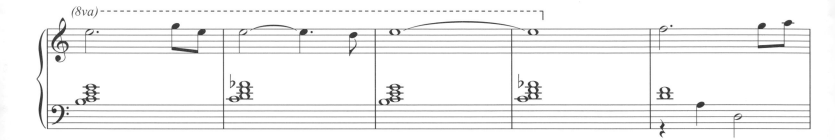

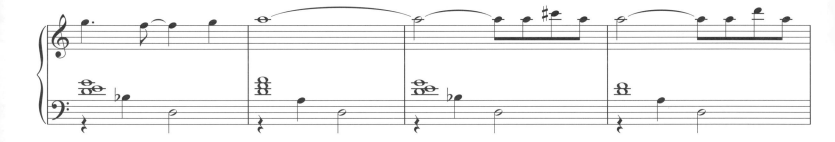

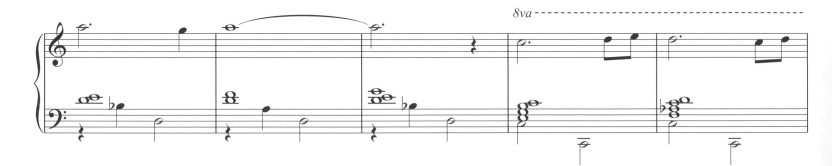

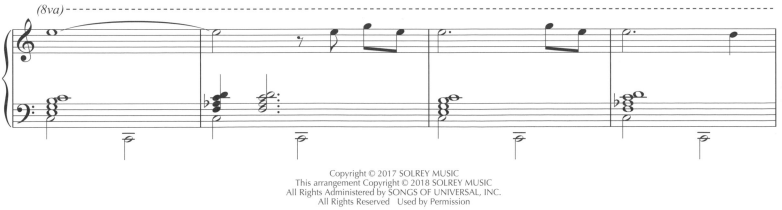

THE ESCAPE

By ALEXANDRE DESPLAT

Slowly, steadily

p

Pedal ad lib. throughout

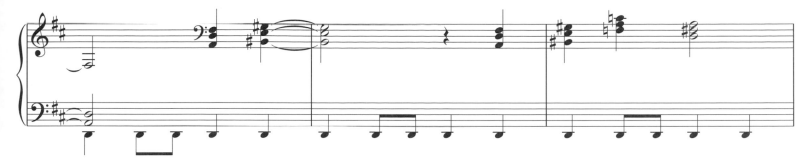

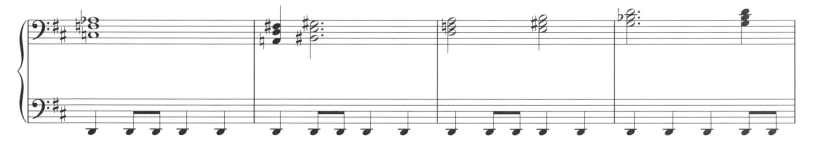

OVERFLOW OF LOVE

By ALEXANDRE DESPLAT

Moderately

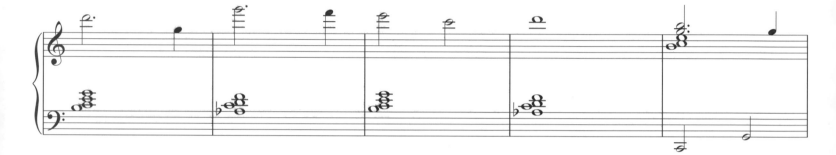

BABALÚ

Words and Music by
MARGARITA LECUONA

lú.

Jun - gle drums were mad - ly beat - ing, ___ in the glare of ee - rie
Ta em - pe - san - do lo ve - lo - rio, ___ que le bu - ce - mo a Ba - ba -

lights ___ while the na - tives kept re - peat - ing ___
lú ___ da - me diez y sie - te ve - las ___

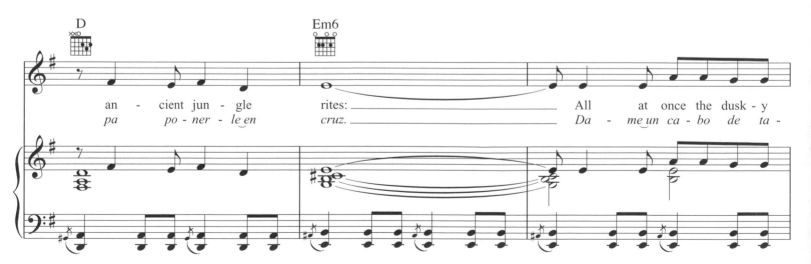

an - cient jun - gle rites: ___ All at once the dusk - y
pa po - ner - le en cruz. ___ Da me un ca - bo de ta -

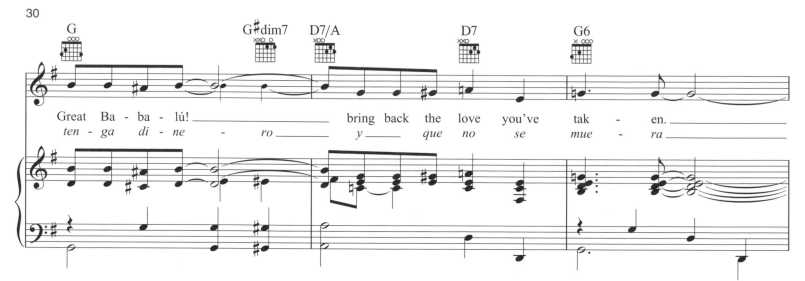

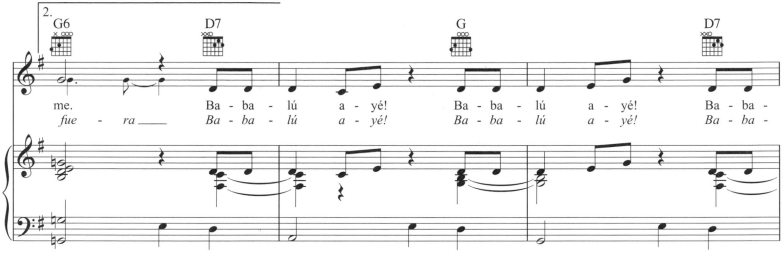

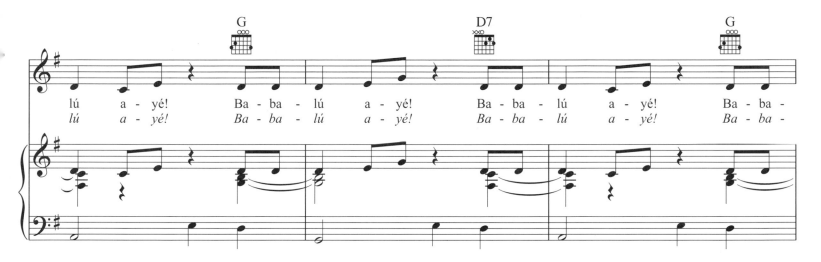

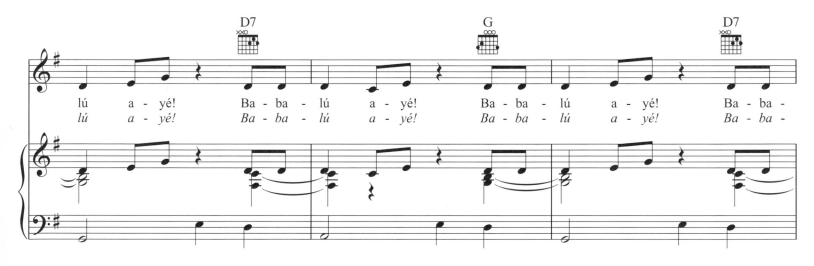

I KNOW WHY
(And So Do You)

Words by MACK GORDON
Music by HARRY WARREN

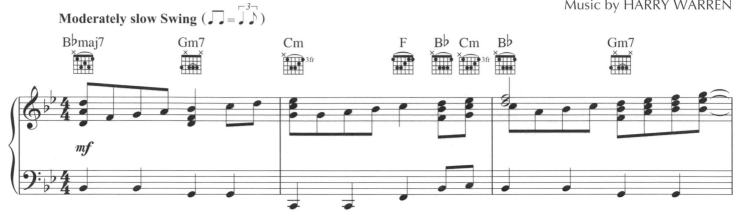

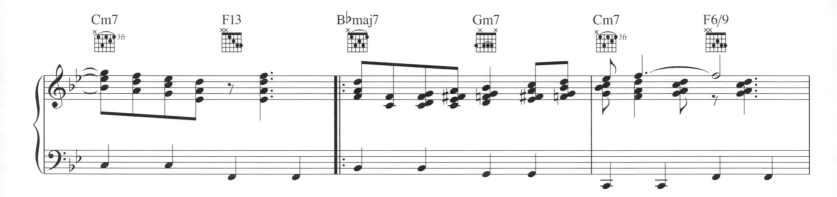

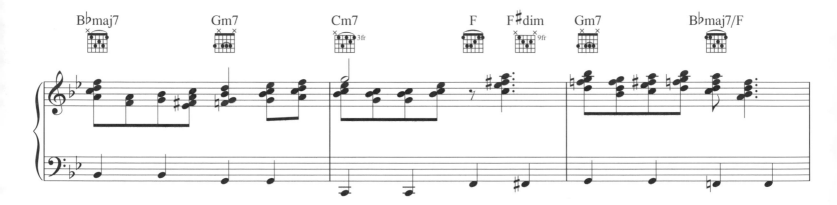

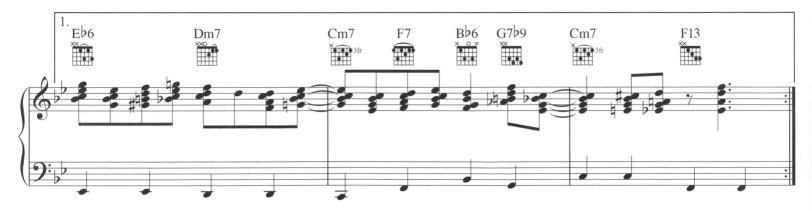

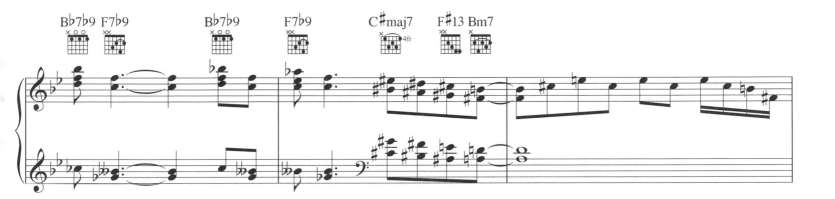

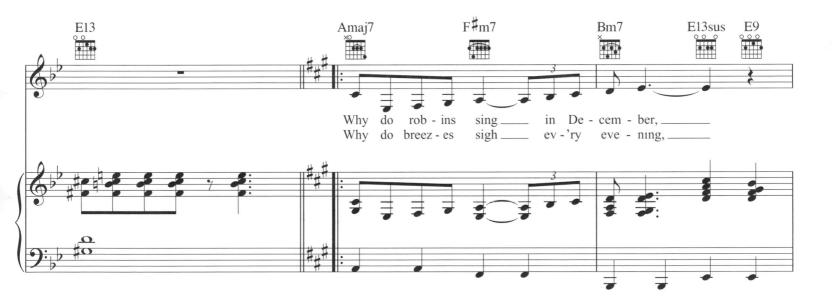

Why do rob - ins sing _____ in De - cem - ber, _____
Why do breez - es sigh _____ ev - 'ry eve - ning, _____

long be - fore the spring - time is due? And, (e - ven though it's snow - ing,
whis - per - ing your name as they do? And,

CHICA CHICA BOOM CHIC

Words by MACK GORDON
Music by HARRY WARREN

Meu co - ra - ção ___ faz chi - ca chi - ca boom chic. ___

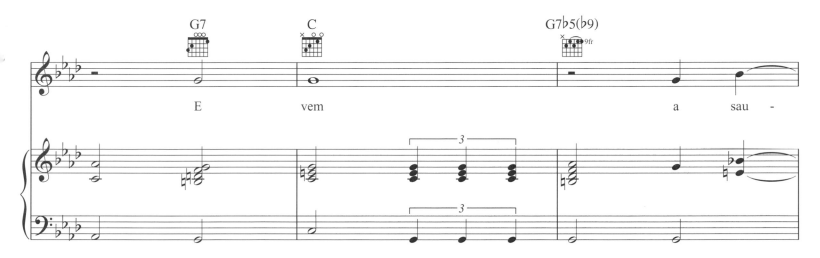

E vem a sau -

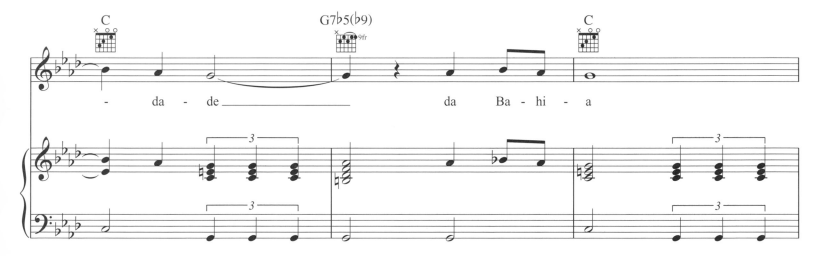

- da - de ___ da Ba - hi - a

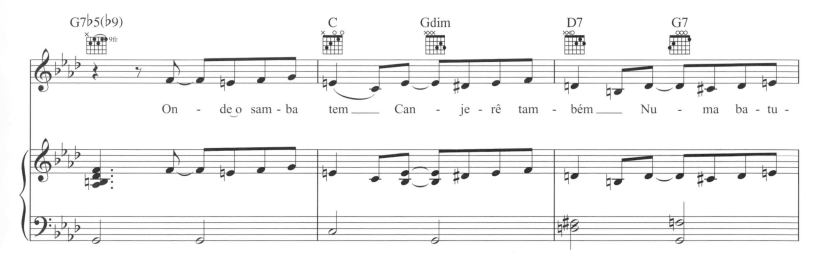

On - de o sam - ba tem ___ Can - je - rê tam - bém ___ Nu - ma ba - tu -

boom chic. _____ E pa - ra

ter - mi - nar. _____ Boom chi - ca chi - ca boom. Vo -

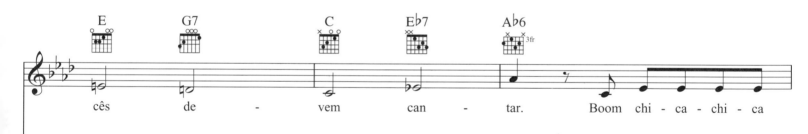

cês de - vem can - tar. Boom chi - ca - chi - ca

boom, chi - ca chi - ca boom, chi - ca chi - ca boom, chi - ca chi - ca boom chic.

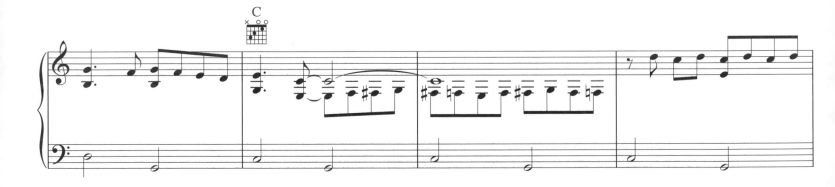

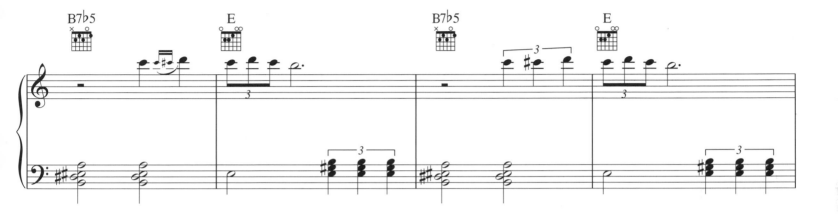

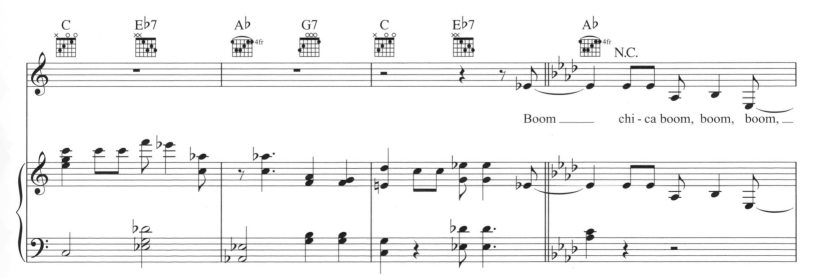

Boom _____ chi - ca boom, boom, boom, _

(Theme from)
A SUMMER PLACE
from A SUMMER PLACE

Words by MACK DISCANT
Music by MAX STEINER

Slowly

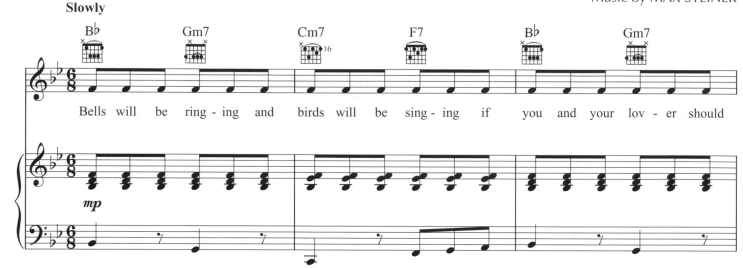

Bells will be ring-ing and birds will be sing-ing if you and your lov-er should

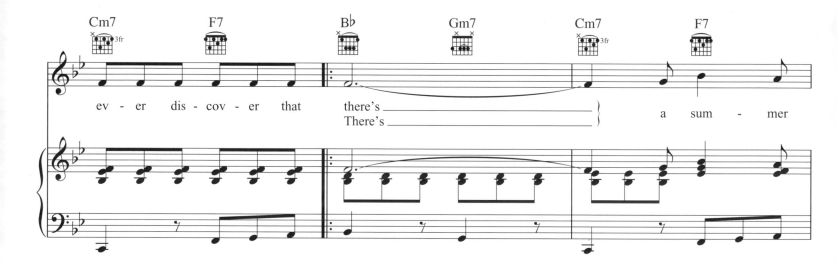

ev - er dis-cov-er that there's _____ } a sum - mer
There's _____

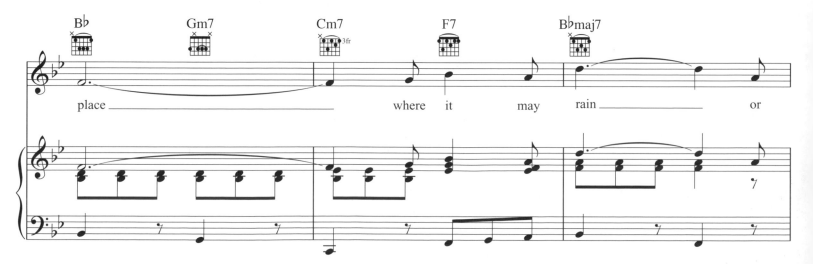

place _____ where it may rain _____ or

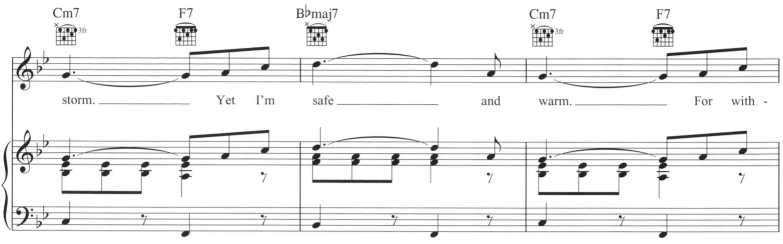

storm. _____ Yet I'm safe _____ and warm. _____ For with -

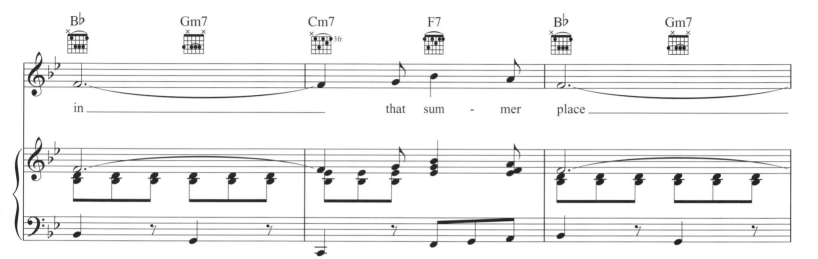

in _____ that sum - mer place _____

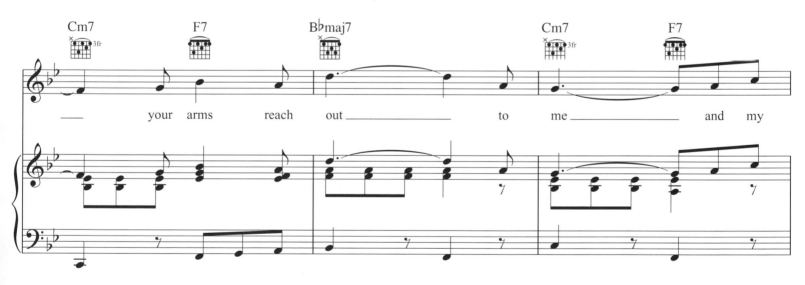

_____ your arms reach out _____ to me _____ and my

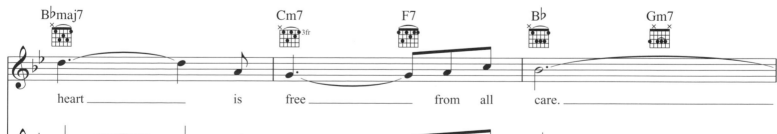

heart _____ is free _____ from all care. _____

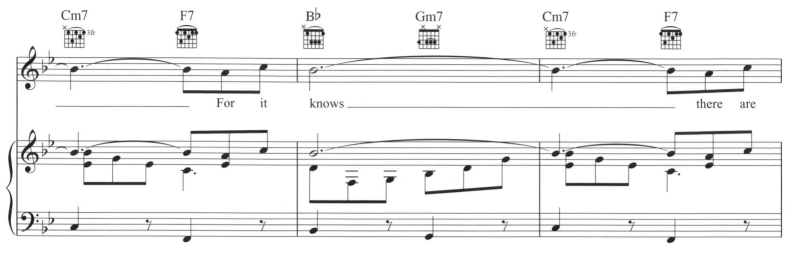

For it knows _____ there are

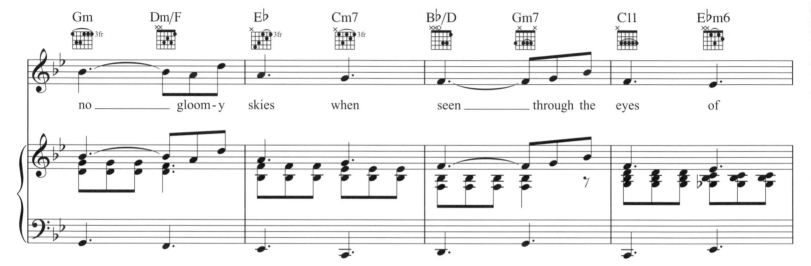

no _____ gloom-y skies when seen _____ through the eyes of

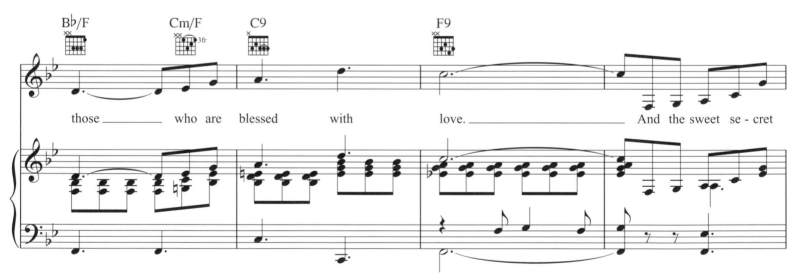

those _____ who are blessed with love. _____ And the sweet se - cret

of _____ a sum - mer place _____ is that it's

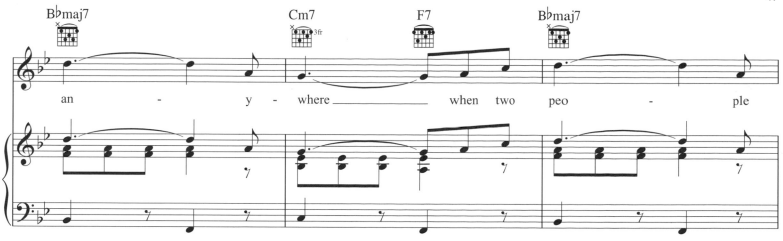

an - y - where _____ when two peo - ple

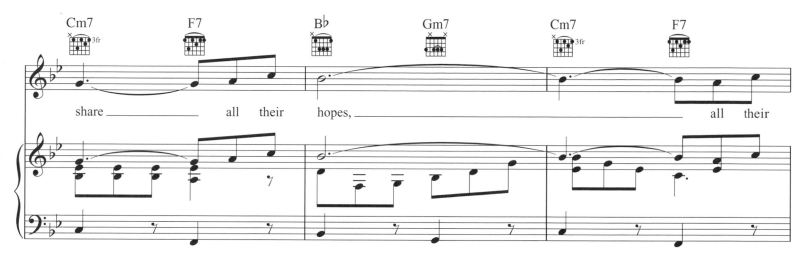

share _____ all their hopes, _____ all their

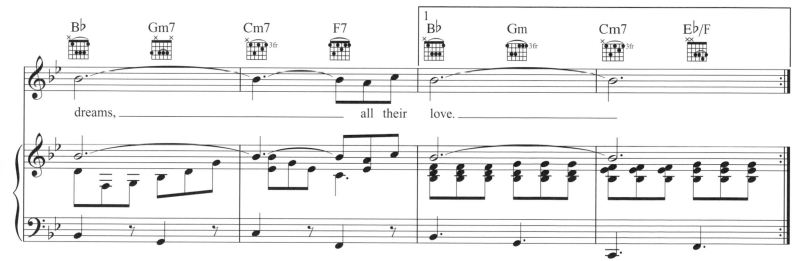

dreams, _____ all their love. _____

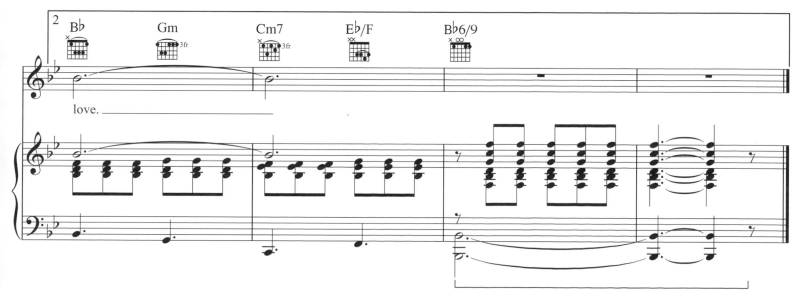

love. _____